Because Nothing Looks Like God

TEACHER'S GUIDE

A Guide for Jewish Educators and Parents

Ideal for Ages 5–8

by Karen Kushner

This Teacher's Guide is the companion to:

11 x 8½, 32 pp
Full-color illus.
Hardcover
ISBN 1-58023-092-X

Also Available:

A gentle way for preschool-age children to explore how God is with us every day, in every way.

To younger children, the world is full of things to see and touch. And by using those very examples, these enchanting books gently invite children to become aware of God's presence all around us.

Abridged from *Because Nothing Looks Like God* by Lawrence and Karen Kushner, these books have been especially adapted in board book format to delight and inspire young readers ages 0–4.

Where Is God?

5 x 5, 24 pp
Full-color illus.
Board Book
ISBN 1-893361-17-9

How Does God Make Things Happen?

5 x 5, 24 pp
Full-color illus.
Board Book
ISBN1-893361-24-1

What Does God Look Like?

5 x 5, 24 pp
Full-color illus.
Board Book
ISBN 1-893361-23-3

Because Nothing Looks Like God
TEACHER'S GUIDE

A Guide for Jewish Educators and Parents

by Karen Kushner

For People of All Faiths, All Backgrounds
JEWISH LIGHTS Publishing

Because Nothing Looks Like God Teacher's Guide

ISBN 978-1-58023-140-4 (pbk.)

ISBN 978-1-68336-740-6 (hc)

Manufactured in the United States of America

For People of All Faiths, All Backgrounds
Published by Jewish Lights Publishing
www.jewishlights.com

Contents

Introduction

It Is Difficult to Talk with Our Kids About God

We read Bible stories to our children and we talk to them about God as part of each holiday season. We even teach them prayers and blessings that are addressed to God. But we often skip the fundamentals, hesitating to begin honest conversations about God because we have yet to replace our own outgrown metaphors. Our childhood images of God are no longer useful, yet we have not found meaningful alternatives. Children are not at all uncomfortable with "God Talk." They ask their innocent questions about everything in their world. It is we, the adults, who get bogged down with doubt and confusion. We ask ourselves: "How can I speak for all of Judaism?" "Am I even sure I believe in God after the Holocaust/AIDS?" "How can I put my spiritual life into words?"

Because Nothing Looks Like God, a book about God for children and adults, makes it possible to begin these conversations. It is a book that speaks of God and spirituality in language that children can understand and adults feel comfortable with. *Because Nothing Looks Like God* takes seriously the spiritual life of children who are beginning to develop their own ideas about God's presence in their lives. It provides words and images for children, their parents, and teachers to continue the exploration of the important truths common to all traditions and to deepen the search for the what, where, and how of God begun by the book.

This *Teacher's Guide* aims to create specific educational opportunities from *Because Nothing Looks Like God.* In it you will find suggested experiences and activities to deepen the search for answers to questions about God begun in the book. This guide also includes topics linking the themes in the book to the Jewish holiday calendar, as well as background information for parents and teachers. The goal of this guide is to provide an ever-deepening spiritual conversation for adults and children in which the beauty and the urgency of children's questions lead to the growth of awe and wonder.

A Few Teaching Ground Rules

With the help of *Because Nothing Looks Like God* and this *Teacher's Guide* you can encourage children to develop their own personal relationship with God.

Remember, *whatever children say about God is true for them.* There are no *wrong* answers. If children's answers are unclear, gently ask them to explain more fully what they are trying to express. Give children a chance to sufficiently articulate their ideas and insist that their peers do the same. In the process of learning about and discussing God, students will also learn to value and respect each other's ideas. Establish a classroom rule that laughter and demeaning comments are not acceptable responses. Allow and encourage all ideas in the discussion. Giving legitimacy to unusual answers will encourage children to think creatively about God. Initially this may prove a more challenging task for parents and teachers than for the children. Many adults experienced an arrested development of their spiritual vocabulary when they were young. *Because Nothing Looks Like God*—both the book and the *Teacher's Guide*—seek to address this disabling tradition and to create a new, open, accepting one in its place. Remember the words of Rabbi Tarfon:

> *It is not your obligation to complete the task, but neither are you free to avoid it* (Pirke Avot *2:16).*

Let us begin a spiritual conversation that can last a lifetime.

How to Use This *Teacher's Guide*

1. Begin with a careful reading of *Because Nothing Looks Like God.* You may even want to jot down a few thoughts or ideas you have as you read it.
2. Each section of the book is allotted a lesson. Prior to the class session, read the lesson and decide which components you will apply in your setting. The elements of each lesson are:
    - A Set Induction or Circle Talk: This introduces the theme of the section of the book. After the Circle Talk, read aloud the assigned section of *Because Nothing Looks Like God* to the class.
    - Project Ideas: Choose activities that are age appropriate. Be sure to make note of the information included in the "Jewish Holiday" and "Judaism and Science" connections and incorporate it into class discussions when applicable.
    - Review the Background Information section and choose the information you want to weave into the lesson.
3. Make it fun!

Notes for Teachers and Parents

To initiate "God Talk" you do not need to be an expert or have all the answers. Asking the question "When do you feel close to God?" acknowledges that God is in our lives and gets the spiritual wheels spinning. There are as many correct answers as there are respondents. You may chose to model for your students by answering truthfully for yourself—"I'm not sure myself. This is what some wise people say.... Sometimes I think...or I feel...." This will allow children to look for their own answers. This will allow them to speak *their* truth.

Lesson I

Where Is God?

Goal: Children will begin to find God in their daily lives.

Introduction

Where is God? This is a natural first question of young children. They have heard their parents and teachers talk about God but feel confused. Bible stories are often introduced to them like fairy tales. They took place "long ago." They contain wonderful occurrences that do not happen in their lives. In contrast, the prayers and blessings they hear imply that God is here today. This seeming contradiction may cause children to react like those who watched the emperor parade naked "in his new clothes" and conclude "but there is no one there!" This lesson addresses the question, "Where is God?"

A. Circle Talk

- Explore students' ideas about holiness and God by asking, "Where is God?" When do you feel close to God? (Remember: Be accepting of everything that any student might say. Do not allow any laughter or dismissal of a student's idea by another student. Endorse the personal nature of each individual's relationship with God.)
- Make four columns on the blackboard that match the four pages of the story: Beginnings, Endings, Family & Friends, Nature. *Do not label the columns* until all the children have responded. Write their responses in the appropriate column or draw simple pictures that illustrate their responses.
- Label the columns Beginnings, Endings, Family & Friends, Nature.

B. Read the section "Where Is God?" in *Because Nothing Looks Like God*

Ask for any additional responses to the question, "Where is God?" Add them to the appropriate column. Show the class how collectively they came to many of the same conclusions as the authors. Point out the responses of the students that match each page. Reinforce for students the idea that by *talking about* God they have let God into their lives.

(Copy the responses from the board and save for further use in Lesson II.)

C. Project Ideas

Preschool: Create a class bulletin board or chart. Each student can add their new God experiences each week. Young children can bring drawings they've made or magazine pictures that illustrate their ideas; add keywords to the students' illustrations for clarity, if needed.

K–1st grade: Each student can make their own *Where Is God?* book of four pages, using the four categories: Beginnings, Endings, Family & Friends, and Nature. Students may add to it every week with drawings, magazine pictures, or photos. Choose one child each week to share his or her book with the class. This will underscore the conclusion that God is everywhere and that it is up to us to let God in.

Connections

Jewish Holiday connection: On Sukkot we leave our big solid houses and live in shaky huts to be close to God in nature. We hold the *lulav* and the *etrog* together to symbolize all of creation. Then we shake them in all six directions to indicate that God is everywhere. God is wherever we let God in.

Judaism and Science connection: A fun way to build awareness of the Jewish connection to nature is to observe the moon. The Jewish calendar is a lunar calendar. Each week, assign a "moon watcher" to observe the moon and report on it to the class. It is easy to tie this to an upcoming holiday as many holidays are in the middle of the month when the moon is full.

D. Background Information for Teachers and Parents

Our tradition teaches that God has an indwelling presence, *Shechinah.* This presence is always close to us. The Jews of sixteenth-century Safed understood that everything contains a spark of the Holy One, Blessed be God. There is a spark of the Divine in every answer. As a matter of fact, the more improbable, the more holy is the vision.

Beginnings

Beginnings are a common theme in our tradition.

- *Rosh HaShanah* is the beginning of the Jewish New Year, the birthday of the year.
- *Bekhor Cholim* are the first fruits that ripen and mark the beginning of the growing season. They are traditionally given to God.
- *Bekhor Reshit* is the first child of a man; and *Peter Rehem* is the first child of a woman.
- *Pidyon HaBen* is the ancient ritual of redeeming the first child.

- *B'Reisheet* is the beginning word of the Torah about the mystery of the beginning of Creation. Usually translated as "In the beginning God created the heavens and the earth," these words from Genesis 1:1 may also be translated as "With *Reisheet* (beginningness), God created the heaven and the earth." *Reisheet* has the same Hebrew root as *Rosh,* meaning "head," or "beginning," or "first."

Endings

Endings are another important theme expressed in Judaism.

- The end of Shabbat is marked by *Havdallah,* the ceremony of distinctions.
- *Shalom* not only means "hello," "good-bye," and "peace," but it also means "ending," in the sense of completeness or wholeness.
- We see those who are at the end of life as being especially worthy for their acquired wisdom.
- We also celebrate the end or completion, the *siyyum,* at the end of a period of study.
- In *Genesis Rabbah* 78:8, we learn that "the last is the most beloved." We read this in the story of Jacob's return to the land of his birth, where his brother Esau lived. Jacob put his wives, Bilhah and Zilpah, and their children in the front of the caravan as it marched toward the dreaded first encounter with Esau. Next came Leah and her children. And the last was Rachel, his most beloved.

Family & Friends

Family and friends are sources of many times of blessing, of drawing close to God.

- At a *bris* or baby naming, family and friends come together to bring the baby into the Jewish community.
- Every Jewish holiday is meant to be celebrated in the context of family and community. We are not meant to be alone in our Jewish celebrations and observances.
- Family, marriage, teacher/student, neighbor to neighbor—all relationships are named in our tradition. Specific rules are listed that help us sanctify the moments that define these important connections and remember God's presence in them (Leviticus).

Nature

Nature is another important path to building our relationship to God.

- At the beginning of the Book of Genesis, the Holy One, Blessed be God, creates all and makes people the caretakers of the world. We have many reminders of this guardianship of nature throughout the year. God intended us to be aware of the movements of the sun and moon in the sky that define our days, weeks, months, and years. These movements form the cycles to which our holidays are tied.

- The sunset and star shine determine the start and end of Shabbat.
- Our holiday calendar is a lunar calendar.
- On Tu B'shvat, we celebrate the New Year of the Trees.
- *S'firat HaOmer,* counting the *omer,* or barley sheaves, is done during the seven weeks between Passover and Shavuot.

Lesson II

What Does God Look Like?

Goal: To build an awareness of non-visual knowing that creates openness to holy moments.

Introduction

Young children are concrete thinkers and long for definite signs of God's presence. Since sight is our dominant sense, this longing is most often expressed with the question, "What does God look like?" When it comes to "seeing" God, confusion is common for children because nothing looks like God and God looks like nothing. "But if God doesn't look like anything, how can I know God is there?" is the inevitable response. This is a wonderful question, a question to bring joy—not terror—to your teaching heart.

One way to address this question is through analogy. Begin with the parent-child relationship. Help students realize that they may know things even when their knowledge is not drawn from visual experience. For example, even when they do not see their parents, they are sure that their parents are in the world. Suggest that students think of times of anxiety when they could not see their parents, such as waking in the night, being in a crowd, attending a sleepover or camp. At these times, often just thinking about their parents reassured them. Remind the children of how we use objects to recall our home and parents. Let them name the objects they use to bring this comfortable feeling. You can then suggest a parallel to the use of ritual objects as comfort objects that connect us to God. The goal is to begin building a vocabulary for children to speak of holy moments, so that they can put these experiences into words. With God, we do not have a visual image in our memory, as we do with parents. Nonetheless, we can have other kinds of sensory memories that remind us of God's reassuring presence in our lives.

A. Circle Talk

Go back to the answers given by the children to the first question, "Where is God?" Ask how the children sensed God was there in the situations they described. Point out that there was nothing to see that *directly* indicated God was present. Help them to recognize that they used feelings of joy or sadness, feelings of connection with another person, wonder or awe. This will provide children with an opportunity to learn keen observation and the need to put things "they just know" into words so that others can share their experiences.

B. Experience

Preschool: Divide the class into groups of four or five students. Blindfold each child in the group. Present one or two of the suggested experiences listed below. After each group has had their experience, have the children come together and share with the entire class what happened to them. Ask them to explain how they knew what the experience was, even though they were blindfolded.

Suggestions for Non-Visual Experiences:

- Feeling of movement of air by fanning a magazine
- Sensing cold from the touch of an ice cube
- Hearing the sound made by crumpling a paper bag
- Hearing the sound of dried beans shaken in a can
- Smelling perfume held under his or her nose
- Smelling pickle juice held under his or her nose

K–1st grade: Set up an "experience station" in the corner of the room or in the hallway of the school. Send students one at a time to the station to be blindfolded and have their experience. Use the same experience for every two or three students. When all the students have returned from the station to the classroom, instruct the children to interview each other. Ask them to find the other or others who had the same experience as they did. Then have each group report on their experiences and all the ways they knew what was happening even though they could not see.

Conclude the discussion of these experiences with the following: People are all different. It is easy to see our physical differences, but we also differ in the way we experience things. For example, point out that not all of the students used the same words to describe their experiences. Listening to each others' descriptions not only shows how we differ, but also helps us open our eyes and give us a broader view of the world around us.

C. Read the section "What Does God Look Like?" in *Because Nothing Looks Like God*

This part of the book reinforces what the children learned in their blindfold experiments. There is no correct answer to the question "What does God look like?" because each person can experience the event differently. One child's experience of time or emotion can be very different from another child's experience. Talk about how someone who loves the beach may find a day short while someone who hates the beach would find the day endless. In just the same way, we can find God present often in our day if we enjoy finding God, while people who do not want relationships with God will not find God. There is nothing to argue about. What is true for one is not experienced by the other. This is often very surprising for children (and adults) who mistakenly assume that everyone experiences the world in the same way. It is very important to not only allow for these differences but to teach children to expect differences and to respect them. This encourages them to share the experiences of their classmates.

D. Project Ideas

Preschool: Make a pinwheel. A pinwheel cannot spin without the wind, but each child can create air movement by dragging the pinwheel through the air or by blowing on it. In the same way, we need to create opportunities for God to be present in our lives.

K–1st grade: Make a videotape of each child showing a page from their God book. Using a VCR, begin playing the tape. First turn off the sound, and then reduce the contrast until the picture disappears. Discuss where the picture goes. Suggest that if we had our eyes focused in just the right way, we could see God more often.

Connections

Jewish Holiday connection: On Shavuot we celebrate God giving us God's Torah.

- Read Deuteronomy 5:4, "The Lord spoke with you face to face at the mountain from the midst of the fire," and Deuteronomy 4:15, "You saw no image when the Lord your God spoke to you at Horeb from out of the fire." These descriptions seem mutually exclusive. One says we saw God face to face and the second reports we saw no image. Emphasize that since the beginning of our relationship with God at Sinai or Horeb, individuals have spoken of their experience of God differently. The Bible, which records the different descriptions, endorses our individuality and makes it part of the God experience. This is one reason why we have different religions today, which are, in fact, different expressions of experiences with the same God. Our memories are different because our experiences of God are different, and the words we choose to describe our experiences can expand that difference.

- There is a midrash that reads as follows: "At the burning bush, God spoke to Moses in the voice of his father. God didn't want to frighten him with a loud voice but God didn't want Moses to be inattentive either" (*Exodus Rabbah* 3:1).

- And from the Torah: "And all the people saw the thunder..." (Exodus 20:15). The experience at Sinai was so powerful that one description has the people seeing sounds, or seeing something that they describe as a sound.

E. Background Information for Teachers and Parents

An old Hasidic story:

> *Once a father and his son were returning home. They came upon a field of blueberries. "Oh, Papa," begged his son, "please can we stop so I can pick some?"*
>
> *"I don't think so. See, it is already growing dark and I am afraid you will become so engrossed in picking berries that you might get lost."*
>
> *Still the little boy persisted, until sometime, as it often happens, a father's resolve is no match for a son's coaxing. "All right, you may pick some berries," the father said, "but only if you will make me a promise. Every few minutes you must stop collecting blueberries and call me. When I hear you calling, I will call back and that way you will know that you are not lost. But listen, my son, the moment you call and I do not answer, you will know that you have gone so far away that I can't even hear you and that you are lost. Then you must forget the blueberries! Then you must call me as loud as you can! And do not stop calling me until you can hear me answer."*

In this story, God is the father and we are the child. What do we need to do to "call God until we hear an answer?"

In her book *Kitchen Table Wisdom,* Rachel Naomi Remen recounts a story of a little girl who had been taught that God watches over us. At first she did not worry because she knew God was there. Then she began to think, what if God blinked? What would happen to her and her world? She was terrified and ran to her grandfather. He asked her, "If you woke up in the night in your room, would you know that your parents were in the house?"

"Yes," she answered.

"How would you know?" her grandfather asked. "Could you see them?"

"No," the little girl responded. She would just know that she wasn't alone in the house.

Lesson III

How Does God Make Things Happen?

Goal: To encourage children to act as God's agents in the world.

Introduction

Children associate miracles with God's presence in the world, and want to know why we do not see miracles today if God is here. Familiarity with Bible stories creates this connection between God and miracles, leaving students to draw the conclusion: no miracles, therefore no God. As teachers, we often point to daily miracles that we can see as evidence of God's presence, such as births, sunrises, rainbows, and recovery from dangerous illness. But children know these are not at all the same as the miracles of the Bible, where the sea split and the sun stood still, where God intervened in history. Those kinds of miracles don't happen anymore. So, they ask, if there is a God, just what does God do and how does God make things happen?

A. Circle Talk

Tell the story of the Garden of Eden (Genesis 1:20–28) and how God created all the animals, leaving Adam and Eve in charge of creation. God told us to take care of God's world. What did this mean? What does it mean in today's world? God has given us a job to do. What happens in your family when people don't do their jobs?

B. Read the section "How Does God Make Things Happen?" in *Because Nothing Looks Like God*

If God is in each of us then it is up to each of us to express God in the world. We have that choice, to express God or not, to choose good or evil. *It is people, not God, who do bad or evil things.* Sometimes people simply forget to be kind. Other times, people do bad things on purpose. Thinking this way helps children to take responsibility for their behavior. It gives them a way to approach others with respect, as they have God in them as well. For young children who often long for super powers, being a part of God, being "God's hands," gives them a glorious sense of their own power to affect things in their universe. Every day, they have opportunities to be God's hands.

C. Project Ideas

Preschool: Imagine you have God's power in your hands. You must pick one thing to do with this "super" power. Give each child a chance to wear a super hero cape and tell how they could use their power to help the world.

K–1st grade: Pick several stories from Danny Segal's *Mitzvah Heroes* and read them to the class. Ask students if they think these events were miracles. Ask them how they think the recipients felt. Did the recipients think it was a miracle? What would make a boy or girl decide to do something like this? Bring a mirror and ask the class if they can see themselves doing a project like the childern in the book. Explore what could be done in these four areas: Family, School, Neighborhood, Town. Pick a class project connected to one of these areas.

Connections

Jewish Holiday connection: Tu B'Shvat is the birthday of the trees and by extension a holiday of ecology and of responsibility for the world.

> *God created man in God's image, in the image of God, God created him, male and female God created them (Genesis 2:7).*

Discuss how each person has the image of God in him or her and how we can train ourselves to see it in others. Encourage the students to find a part of God even in people they don't like. How does this change their feelings about these people?

D. Background Information for Teachers and Parents

There is a mystical creation story about sparks of God trapped in each of us, based on the teachings of Isaac Luria of thirteenth-century Safed:

Before the world
there was only the Holy One
filling all space and all time.
Everything was part of the One
blended together,
with no beginning and no end.

The Holy One
took a deep breath
became smaller and smaller
to make space and time.
And for the first time,
there was a place where the Holy One was not.

Into that nothing space

the Holy One spun rays of light,
weaving ten shining threads
as if one candle lit another,
bright as the sun,
warm as a burning coal.

Sparks of the Holy One
fell from above
became trapped in us.
Look,
you can see the glow
a faint glimmer reflecting their holy source.

—Karen Kushner

Conclusion

Each of the stories in *Because Nothing Looks Like God* speaks honestly to children about the possibility of perceiving the presence of the Holy One in the world, without insisting on one particular way. Each story is designed to open doors, to develop a vocabulary, to begin a conversation that includes everyone's experiences. *Because Nothing Looks Like God* not only provides a way into that dialogue but it also helps children understand that holiness and the experience of God in our lives come in different ways. It is only a small step to seeing that different symbols and different songs are only expressions of the commonality of religious experience.

Printed in the USA
CPSIA information can be obtained
at www.ICGtesting.com
JSHW060049150824
68134JS00031B/2699

9 781580 231404